Zlatka Koleva

Directive 1999/44/EC and the Smart Regulation

Has the Directive complied with the principles of simplicity and proportionality under the Smart Regulation initiative for consumers in Germany and England and Wales?

Anchor Academic
Publishing

Koleva, Zlatka: Directive 1999/44/EC and the Smart Regulation: Has the Directive complied with the principles of simplicity and proportionality under the Smart Regulation initiative for consumers in Germany and England and Wales?
Hamburg, Anchor Academic Publishing 2015

Buch-ISBN: 978-3-95489-334-8
PDF-eBook-ISBN: 978-3-95489-834-3
Druck/Herstellung: Anchor Academic Publishing, Hamburg, 2015

Bibliografische Information der Deutschen Nationalbibliothek:
Die Deutsche Nationalbibliothek verzeichnet diese Publikation in der Deutschen Nationalbibliografie; detaillierte bibliografische Daten sind im Internet über http://dnb.d-nb.de abrufbar.

Bibliographical Information of the German National Library:
The German National Library lists this publication in the German National Bibliography. Detailed bibliographic data can be found at: http://dnb.d-nb.de

All rights reserved. This publication may not be reproduced, stored in a retrieval system or transmitted, in any form or by any means, electronic, mechanical, photocopying, recording or otherwise, without the prior permission of the publishers.

Das Werk einschließlich aller seiner Teile ist urheberrechtlich geschützt. Jede Verwertung außerhalb der Grenzen des Urheberrechtsgesetzes ist ohne Zustimmung des Verlages unzulässig und strafbar. Dies gilt insbesondere für Vervielfältigungen, Übersetzungen, Mikroverfilmungen und die Einspeicherung und Bearbeitung in elektronischen Systemen.

Die Wiedergabe von Gebrauchsnamen, Handelsnamen, Warenbezeichnungen usw. in diesem Werk berechtigt auch ohne besondere Kennzeichnung nicht zu der Annahme, dass solche Namen im Sinne der Warenzeichen- und Markenschutz-Gesetzgebung als frei zu betrachten wären und daher von jedermann benutzt werden dürften.

Die Informationen in diesem Werk wurden mit Sorgfalt erarbeitet. Dennoch können Fehler nicht vollständig ausgeschlossen werden und die Diplomica Verlag GmbH, die Autoren oder Übersetzer übernehmen keine juristische Verantwortung oder irgendeine Haftung für evtl. verbliebene fehlerhafte Angaben und deren Folgen.

Alle Rechte vorbehalten

© Anchor Academic Publishing, Imprint der Diplomica Verlag GmbH
Hermannstal 119k, 22119 Hamburg
http://www.diplomica-verlag.de, Hamburg 2015
Printed in Germany

Table of Contents

Preface 1

Introduction 2

Chapter 1: Article 3 and 5 of Directive 1999/44/EC 5

Section 1: Legal basis 5

Section 2: Article 3 of the Consumer Rights Directive 6

Section 3: Article 5 of the Consumer Rights Directive 7

Section 4: Interpretation of article 3 in the light of the case-law of the European Court of Justice 7

Section 5: Conclusion 9

Chapter 2: The German domestic order and the legal transposition of articles 3 and 5 of the Consumer Rights Directive 10

Section 1: Legal historical developments in German civil law 10

Section 2: The legal shift from Waldung and Minderung to Nacherfüllung – implementation of article 3 of the Consumer Rights Directive into German law 11

Section 3: From six months to two years – implementation of article 5 into the German legal order 12

Section 4: Conclusion 14

Chapter 3: The English common law system and the legal transposition of articles 3 and 5 of the Consumer Rights Directive 16

Section 1: Common law rules under the Sale of Goods Act 16

Section 2: Implementation of articles 3 and 5 of the Consumer Rights Directive in the Sale of Goods Act 17

Section 3: Conclusion 18

Chapter 4: Legal analysis of the implementation effects of articles 3 and 5 of the Consumer Rights Directive into the domestic legal systems of Germany and England and Wales 20

Section 1: Implementation effects of articles 3 and 5 of the Consumer Rights Directive on the German civil law system 21

Subsection 1: Violation of article 3 of the Consumer Rights Directive and the principles of simplicity and proportionality of the Smart Regulation 21

Subsection 2: Article 5 of the Consumer Rights Directive and its adherence to the principles of simplicity and proportionality under the Smart Regulation 24

Subsection 3: Interdependence of articles 3 and 5 of the Consumer Rights Directive 25

Subsection 4: Conclusion... 26

Section 2: Implementation effects of articles 3 and 5 of the Consumer Rights Directive within the English common law order 26

Subsection 1: Potential issues with article 3 of the Consumer Rights Directive 27

Subsection 2: Primary common law rule of the six-year limitation period 29

Subsection 3: Conclusion 30

Section 3: Summary 30

Concluding remarks 31

Germany 31

England and Wales 33

Directive 1999/44/EC 35

Conclusion 39

Summary 39

Annex I 40
Bibliography 42

Preface

Almost twenty-five exams passed, over a hundred pages written for assignments and seminars, having lived in three European cities in two different European countries before turning the age of 22, made an Erasmus exchange in the United Kingdom, 2222 kilometers away from my home city, after countless struggles and restlessness nights spent studying, three years later I have never been nearer to fulfilling my biggest dream – to be an International and European law lawyer. On the final line, I would like to devote this page to those who helped me write this book.

My warm gratitude goes to my thesis supervisor, Mr. Lorenzo Squintani for his commitment, devotion and constant support, without which I would have been left blindfolded. I must admit that his high expectations I had to live up to have challenged me to push myself to the limit and improved the quality of my paper. A simple 'thank you' would not be enough.

This would not have ever existed without Lia Trenovska, who was the fountain of inspiration to me throughout the whole process. She was always there when I needed her, gave me advice and supported me all the way through. A colleague, a friend, my better half.

I am deeply thankful to Prof. Dr. Michael Jänsch, professor at Hochschule für Technik und Wirtschaft Berlin, for his expert advice and guidance into the depths of German civil law, which contributed to my better understanding of the intersection between the law of obligations in Germany and the European order.

To my Erasmus roommate and colleague – Maria Søs Schultz, who proved me that Erasmus makes connections forever. Thank you for the tons of valuable information on English commercial law you provided me with, when I needed it the most.

Finally, a heartfelt gratitude to my wonderful family and friends, who, regardless of the long distance, managed to cheer me up and pour strength and positive energy on me. I have never let you down and this would not be an exception.

Introduction

From the birth of the European Economic Community as an autonomous economically-driven organization aiming at regulation of the internal market in Europe to its very official establishment as a Union,[1] the European Union has played a crucial role in the dynamic economic, social and political affairs not only on the continent, but also worldwide as a patron of European legal traditions. In this respect, modernization and globalization encourage significant legal developments to occur, reshaping the current normative framework. Thus, the European Union as a main actor on the international legal scene had to restructure its legal order, namely European law,[2] in order to adapt new changes and relate them in a coherent way with its values and principles.[3]

This has been demonstrated by the initiation of the Smart Regulation in October 2010.[4] It is a successor of the Better Regulation initiative launched in 2002 and repealed in 2006, which aims to simplify the law, repeal outdated legislative acts, reduce regulatory burden through regulatory fitness checks and benefit people and businesses, in particular small and medium enterprises.[5] In this paper two of these principles will be discussed in more detail, simplicity and proportionality respectively. On the one hand, simplicity implies that a regulation should be as simple as possible and as detailed as necessary.[6] Such a concept urges for simple wording and, occasionally, requires a degree of detail for the principle of necessity; its primary goal remains combatting excessive detail in the drafting process for the purposes of clarity and correct implementation of EU law.[7] Proportionality, on the other, is a deeply-rooted principle in EU law, which provides that any Union action shall not exceed what is found necessary to

---

[1] Treaty on European Union, as amended by the Maastricht Treaty (1992) OJ C 191.
[2] The President of the European Commission – José Barroso stated that "European law is at the heart of what makes the European Union special" in 'Better Regulation – simply explained', 1.
[3] Lisbon European Council, *Presidency Conclusions* (2000) para.1.
[4] IP/10/1296 (2010).
[5] ibid.; See also COM (2010) 543 final; COM (2013) 685 final 1-5; Alina Kaczorowska, *European Union Law* (Routledge 2013) 154; Wolfgang Kowalsky and Peter Scherrer (ed), *Trade unions for a change of course in Europe* (ETUI 2011) 111; Adam Cygan, *Accountability, Parliamentarism and Transparency in the EU* (Edward Elgar Publishing 2013) 56; Tony Prosser, *The Regulatory Enterprise: Government, Regulation, and Legitimacy* (Oxford University Press 2010) 80.
[6] Mandelkern Group on Better Regulation (2001) 10.
[7] ibid. 67.

achieve the objectives of the Treaties.[8] Thus, the Union shall strike a balance between the rights it gives and the constraints it imposes for the purposes of EU law.[9] The choice to combine simplicity and proportionality as two corners of a normative legal framework is not coincidental: simplicity embraces simple and clear wording of EU law rules and, if this rule is kept intact, the implemented rules would lead to proportionate outcomes to European citizens. For this reason, their interrelation deserves to be paid a closer attention.

The European Commission already outlined the importance of the interdependence of these two principles; in a Commission Staff Working Paper focused on monitoring and consultation of small and medium enterprises (SMEs) in March 2013 European organizations admitted the burdensome character of some aspects of Directive 1999/44/EC on the sale of consumer goods and associated guarantees on consumers.[10] As a result, the Commission suggested that the solution thereof would be to consolidate and simplify the law on consumer protection as to ensure more effective rights for consumers;[11] additionally, social campaigns such as the Consumer Rights Awareness Campaign aim to promote consumer protection and inform citizens of their rights within the Union.[12]

For this reason, this legal challenge is the focus of this paper, in particular articles 3 and 5 of the Consumer Rights Directive, respectfully on the newly adopted system of remedies and the imposed two-year warranty period. Furthermore, a closer insight into the application of these provisions of the Directive in two legal regimes will be provided, on the one hand Germany, being a classical example of a straight-forward civil law system, and on the other England and Wales as part of the well-established common law tradition. In conclusion, a short summary of possible improvements with

---

[8] Consolidated Version of the Treaty on European Union (2008) OJ C 115/13 article 5, para.4; See also COM (2010) 547 final.
[9] Mandelkern Group on Better Regulation (n 6) 9.
[10] SWD (2013) 60 final at 17, 19, 22 and 24.
[11] COM (2013) 685 final (n 5) 7; Annex to COM (2013) 685 final 5.
[12] Consumer Rights Awareness Campaign has been organized by the EU Commission and it is running from from 17.03.to 31.12.2014 in order to raise awareness among consumers about their rights and obligations under EU law. For more detailed information, visit http://ec.europa.eu/justice/newsroom/consumer-marketing/event/140317_en.htm (accessed 10 March 2014).

regard to the German, English and European order will be provided in order to ensure a higher level of legal certainty and consumer protection.

Thus, the research question of this thesis concerns whether the Consumer Rights Directive complies with the principles of simplicity and proportionality within the Smart Regulation normative framework as applied in Germany and England and Wales. For this purpose, the three legal orders will be discussed separately: EU, German and English consumer law, followed by an analysis of the application of articles 3 and 5 of the Directive into these two national legal orders and their implications in the light of the principles of simplicity and proportionality under the Smart Regulation. At the end of this paper, concluding remarks will be made based on the conclusions of the analysis as to whether or not the application of this directive provides high level of protection and, thus, legal certainty to consumers and suggestions will be provided for the improvement and harmonization of the future EU consumer law order and its intersection with national traditions.

Throughout this research I have consulted work of academic writers and lawyers, papers and communications, as well as annexes and initiated investigations, parliamentary discussions, explanatory notes, EU legislation, case law of the German Supreme Court, the European Court of Justice and reports of the Law Commission in the UK and Scotland. In addition, I have consulted Dr. Michael Jänsch, professor in German civil law, for further clarification and a better understanding of the law of obligations in Germany.

Chapter 1: Article 3 and 5 of Directive 1999/44/EC

The starting point of this paper would logically be the Consumer Rights Directive, as it lies in the heart of the discussion.[1] A brief discussion on the legal basis of the Directive will be provided and then reader's attention will be focused on two specific articles, namely article 3 and 5, referring to the newly proposed remedial system and the two-year warranty period. Finally, a short summary of relevant case-law of the European Court of Justice ("the ECJ") in relation to these provisions, in particular article 3, will be included in order to illustrate the court's interpretation of the Directive with regard to its application and interpretation on national level.

Section 1: Legal basis

The Consumer Rights Directive itself refers to article 169 [ex article 153 TEC] of the Treaty on the Functioning of the European Union as a legal source, which promotes high level of protection for consumers.[2] This concept has been further embraced by the drafters, as recitals 1 and 23 demonstrate.[3] An important remark would be that this rule is applicable pursuant to article 114 [ex article 95 TEC] of the same Treaty, which envisages the ground-laying idea of the Directive as a whole to serve as a means for minimum harmonization;[4] the intent of the legislator seems to have adopted this line of thought judging by several recitals.[5] Thus, based on the principles embedded in the Treaties, the Consumer Rights Directive should be interpreted as a tool for

---

[1] Directive 1999/44/EC of the European Parliament and of the Council of 25 May 1999 on certain aspects of the sale of consumer goods and associated guarantees [hereinafter referred as "The Directive"].
[2] Consolidated version of the Treaty on the Functioning of the European Union [hereinafter referred as "TFEU"] (2008) C 115/01 article 169, para. 1.
[3] Recital 1 and 23 of the Directive refer to the substantial contribution of the Community for the achievement of a higher level of protection, which is considered a growing concern in the light of EU law.
[4] ibid. recital 1; TFEU (n 2) article 114, paras. 4-5; See also Iris Benöhr, *EU Consumer Law and Human Rights* (Oxford University Press 2013) 31; Stephen Weatherill, 'Maximum versus Minimum Harmonization: Choosing between Unity and Diversity in the Search of the Soul of the Internal Market' in Niamh Shuibhne and Laurence Gormley (ed), *From Single Market to Economic Union: Essays in Memory of John A. Usher* (Oxford University Press 2012) 182-183; Hans-W. Micklitz, 'Federal Order of Competence and Private Law' in Loïc Azoulai (ed), *The Question of Competence in the European Union* (Oxford University Press 2014) 148.
[5] Recitals 2 and 5 of the Directive refer to a 'minimum set of fair values'/ 'minimum rules of consumer law', whereas recital 4 straight-forwardly asserts the dominant concern of an absence of minimum harmonization with regard to consumer law rules.

minimum harmonization in its transposition to national law orders, since it provides member states with the open opportunity to impose stricter rules on specific areas.[6]

Section 2: Article 3 of the Consumer Rights Directive

One of the main points of discussion in this paper is the newly adopted system of remedies under article 3 of the Directive. The provision itself lays its basis on the principle that the seller is responsible for any lack of conformity on his behalf with regard to the goods delivered.[7] However, the Directive provides an opportunity for specific performance for the seller to repair or replace the faulty good free of charge or either to reduce the price of the good or to have the contract terminated with regard to the good.[8] As it can be observed from this provision, the Consumer Rights Directive imposes a strict hierarchy of remedies available under the EU regime: the first trier of remedies is repair or replacement, unless it is found impossible or disproportionate.[9] For this purpose, a disproportionality test is implemented to help the seller determine which one of the two remedies to choose, depending on the initial value of the goods, the degree of the lack of conformity and assessing whether an alternative remedy would be more convenient for the consumer.[10] Moreover, both repair and replacement should be performed within a reasonable time period and shall not be detrimental to the convenience of the consumer.[11] In case both options under the first trier are found either impossible or disproportionate, the consumer should have access to the second trier of relief, namely reduction of price or termination of contract. As it seems, the newly adopted set of rules with regard to remedies appears to be a straight-forward system with reasonable amount of detail for the purpose of clarity.

---

[6] Recital 7 resembles the rule adopted in para.5 of article 114 of the Directive.
[7] The Directive (n 1) article 3, para. 1.
[8] ibid. para. 2.
[9] ibid. para.3.
[10] ibid.
[11] ibid.

Section 3: Article 5 of the Consumer Rights Directive

Pursuant to article 3, another central issue is the uniform set limitation period for lodging a claim due to lack of conformity on behalf of the seller with regard to any faulty goods delivered, which according to article 5 of the Directive lasts two years.[12] The provision also refers to an open legal possibility for member states to oblige the consumer to inform the seller of any lack of conformity of the goods within the period of two months from the date of delivery;[13] however, the usage of the word '*may*' in the provision implies that the choice to enforce it lies with the will of the legislator of each member state. Furthermore, under paragraph 3 of the article in question any lack of conformity with the good within six months from the date of delivery is presumed to have existed from the beginning.[14] Nonetheless, for the purposes of this research, this paper emphasizes only on the legal implications of article 5, paragraph 1 with regard to the timeframe for claims, which varies from two, as in Germany for instance, to six years in England and Wales, since member states are allowed to impose stringent rules for a higher level of consumer protection.[15]

Section 4: Interpretation of article 3 in the light of the case-law of the European Court of Justice

The case-law of the European Court of Justice ("the ECJ") has explored a legal vacuum, in particular in relation to article 3 of the Directive. One of the most important cases for its correct interpretation with regard to the newly adopted remedial system as implemented into national legal orders is considered to be the *Quelle AG v Bundesverband der Verbrauchzentralen und Verbraucherverbände* case ("Quelle AG").[16] The German legislator adopted article 3 into the domestic legal order, leaving the consumer responsible for covering expenses for the usage of a faulty good, an interpre-

---

[12] ibid. article 5, para. 1.
[13] ibid. para. 2.
[14] Article 5, para.3 of the Directive refers to the nature of both the good and the lack of conformity as the only exceptions of this rule.
[15] The Directive (n 1) recital 24 and article 8, para. 2; See generally Nicolas Ryder et al, *Commercial Law: Principles and Policy* (Cambridge University Press 2012); Eric Baskind et al, *Commercial Law* (Oxford University Press 2013) 446.
[16] Case C-404/06 *Quelle AG v Bundesverband der Verbraucherzentralen und Verbraucherverbände* ECR I-2685 [hereinafter referred as "Quelle AG"].

tation which the ECJ contested. The discussion in this case highlights the importance of the general and underlying principle under article 3, paragraph 1 that the seller is initially responsible for any lack of conformity of the delivered goods;[17] furthermore, the court reiterated that regardless of the choice of a remedy under article 3, paragraph 3, either repair or replacement, the term *'free of charge'* within this provision is not coincidental: its function is to reflect "the intention of the Community legislature to strengthen consumer protection".[18] The most relevant conclusion of this case would be that the consumer should not pay for the usage of a faulty good.[19]

Judging by the recent case-law of the ECJ, article 3 seems to be ambiguous in its wording and, thus, in its application into domestic legal systems and national courts appear to have been faced with a legal lacuna in the Directive. In this respect, another case in point would be the joined case *Gebr. Weber GmbH/Ingrid Putz* ("Gebr. Weber/Ingrid Putz").[20] Due to misinterpretation on behalf of the German legislators when adopting article 3 into the national legal framework, the disproportionality rule embedded in this provision has been expanded in two dimensions, implying two different scenarios which can be taken into account: relative and absolute proportionality. Applying the former, repair and replacement are weighted against each other and in the case of the latter, even one of both remedies is available, it should not be granted in case its application would amount to great and excessive disproportionality to the detriment of the seller.[21] However, this line of interpretation has been rejected by the ECJ, arguing

---

[17] ibid. 26.
[18] ibid. 30.
[19] ibid. 43. See also Hannes Rösler, *Europäische Gerichtsbarkeit auf dem Gebiet des Zivilrechts* (Mohr Siebeck 2012) 162; Christian Twigg-Flesner, *The Europeanisation of Contract Law: Current Controversies in Law* (Routledge 2013) 108; Christian Twigg-Flesner, 'Fit for purpose? The Proposals on Sales' in Geraint Howells and Reiner Schulze (ed), *Modernising and Harmonising Consumer Contract Law* (Selier Europeal Law Publishers 2009) 170; Stephen Weatherill, 'Consumer Policy' in Paul P. Craig, Gráinne De Búrca (ed), *The Evolution of EU Law* (Oxford University Press 2011) 859; Peter Rott, "Technical Harmonization' versus Substantive Differences' in Alessandro Somma (ed), *The Politics of the Draft Common Frame of Reference* (Kluwer Law International 2009) 172; See generally Ulrich Magnus, 'Consumer sales and associated guarantees' in Christian Twigg-Flesner (ed), *The Cambridge Companion to European Union Private Law* (Cambridge University Press 2010).
[20] Joined Cases C-65/09 and C-97/09 *Gebr.Weber GmbH v Jürgen Wittmer, and Ingrid Putz v Medianess Electronics GmbH* [2011] ECR I-5257 [hereinafter referred to as "Gebr. Weber"].
[21] Christian Twigg-Flesner, *The Europeanisation of Contract Law: Current Controversies in Law* (n 19); Deutscher Bundestag, Drucksache 14/6040, 219-220; See also Florian Faust, 'Das Kaufrecht im Vorschlag für ein Gemeinsames Europäisches Kaufrecht' in Hans Schulte-Nölke et al (ed), *Der Entwurf für ein optionales europäisches Kaufrecht* (Selier European law Publishers 2012) 258.

that it would deprive the consumer of a short-term remedy.[22] Furthermore, such practice would contradict with the aim of the Directive to provide a high level of consumer protection.[23] According to the court's reasoning, if the only available remedy is not impossible, then it has to be granted to the consumer at expense of the seller, thus, the relative disproportionality test was favoured.[24] As it can be deduced by *Gebr. Weber/Ingrid Putz* ruling, the notion of legal expectations of non-faulty goods finds its roots in the very core of the right to consumer protection, which corresponds directly to the line of argumentation in the *Quelle AG* case, where the '*free of charge*' principle prevailed on this ground.[25]

Section 5: Conclusion

In conclusion, it can be summarized that articles 3 and 5, respectfully in relation to remedies and the two-year limitation period for claims, raise additional questions with regard to their application into national law orders, as demonstrated by the ECJ case-law developments, such as *Quelle AG* and *Gebr. Weber/Ingrid Putz*. In order to identify these legal gaps it should first be made a brief introduction into the two separate legal frameworks this paper focuses on, namely the German civil law system and the English common law order.

---

[22] Gebr. Weber (n 20) 65.
[23] ibid.
[24] ibid. 68.
[25] ibid. 46, 49-53; Quelle AG (n 16) 33-34; See also n 19.

Chapter 2: The German domestic order and the legal transposition of articles 3 and 5 of the Consumer Rights Directive

The discussion on the Quelle AG[1] and Gebr. Weber/Ingrid Putz[2] cases logically is followed by a short introduction to the German legal norms as affected by the implementation of the Consumer Rights Directive[3]. For this purpose, the major significance of this piece of EU legislation will be illustrated in relation to the foundation of contemporary German civil law rules resulted in the newly adopted version of the German civil code (Bürgerliches Gesetzbuch, "the BGB"). Therefore, special attention will be drawn to sections 437, 438 and 439 of the BGB, which mirror articles 3 and 5 of the Directive. In conclusion, a reference will be made to the legal inconsistencies between the formulation of the German legislators and the wording of the Directive, problems which will be discussed in detail in Chapter 4.

Section 1: Legal historical developments in German civil law

The debates in Germany about a radical reform in civil law date from 1979, when an initiative was undertaken by the Minister of Justice to issue a report on German contract law.[4] After the unification and the establishment of the Federal Republic of Germany, a Commission Reforming the Law of Obligations recalled the need for a new order and referred to the fore-mentioned commissioned study;[5] the efforts of the Commission resulted in an extensive report, but it did not lead to any initiative by the legislator. It was not until the millennium a reform of the German civil code appeared on the agenda, when the competitive struggle in cross-border transactions became

---

[1] Case C-404/06 *Quelle AG v Bundesverband der Verbraucherzentralen und Verbraucherverbände* [2008] ECR I-2685.
[2] Joined Cases C-65/09 and C-97/09 *Gebr.Weber GmbH v Jürgen Wittmer, and Ingrid Putz v Medianess Electronics GmbH* [2011] ECR I-5257.
[3] Directive 1999/44/EC of the European Parliament and of the Council of 25 May 1999 on certain aspects of the sale of consumer goods and associated guarantees [hereinafter referred to as "The Directive"] OJ L 171.
[4] Peter Pott and Christian Twigg-Flesner, 'No Closer to Harmonisation? The Implementation of Directive 1999/44/EC into English and German Law Three Years On' in Geraint Howells et al (ed), *The Yearbook of Consumer Law 2007* (Publisher 2007) 122; See also Ulrich Huber in BMJ (ed), *Gutachten und Vorschläge zur Überarbetung des Schulrechts* (Bundesanzeiger Verlag, 1981); Yoshio Shiomi, 'Modernization of German Civil Law' in Zentaro Kitagawa and Karl Riesenhuber (ed), *The Identity of German and Japanese Civil Law in Comparative Perspectives/Die Identität des Deutschen und des Japanischen Zilivrechts in vergleichender Betrachtung* (De Gruyter Rechtswissenschaften Verlags – GmbH 2007) 67.
[5] ibid.

apparent and called for a legislative change.⁶ There were also practical reasons for Germany to undertake such action, such as the simultaneous implementation of three European Directives, namely the Consumer Sales and Associated Guarantees Directive, the Directive on Late Payments and the Directive on Electronic Commerce.⁷ Moreover, the Minister of Justice at that time – Prof. Dr. Herta Däubler-Gmelin, expressed her concern that a failure to compile the law would inevitably cause complications in its application, since four different sets of rules – the three Directives and the former German civil code, have to be applied simultaneously.⁸ Furthermore, as the time for implementation of the Consumer Sales and Associated Guarantees Directive expired on 31 December 2001, this served as an impetus for the German Bundesrat to radically reconsider the German civil law approach.⁹

Section 2: The legal shift from Waldung and Minderung to Nacherfüllung – implementation of article 3 of the Consumer Rights Directive into German law

The German law of obligations before 2002 was heavily influenced by old Roman law traditional principles, for instance the right to direct revocation of a contract (*Waldung*).¹⁰ It refers to the *warranty* theory (*Gewährleistungstheorie*), which empowered the consumer to directly return the good to the seller and request a reduction of price (*Minderung*).¹¹ However, this exclusive right rested with the consumer only upon delivery.¹² While such practice places the buyer indisputably in a very disadvantageous

---

⁶ Peer Zumbansen, 'The Law of Contracts' in Mathias Reimann and Joachim Zekoll (ed), *Introduction to German Law* (Kluwer Law International 2005) 201.
⁷ The Directive (n 3); Directive 2000/35/EC of the European Parliament and the Council of 29 June 2000 on combating late payment in commercial transactions OJ L 200; Directive 2000/31/EC of the European Parliament and of the Council of 8 June 2000 on certain legal aspects of information society services, in particular electronic commerce, in the internal market OJ L 178; Deutscher Bundestag, 166. Sitzung, 16213 (B).
⁸ ibid. 161215 (A).
⁹ ibid.; See also Peter Pott and Christian Twigg-Flesner (n 4); Yoshio Shiomi (n 4) 67-71; Peer Zumbansen (n 6).
¹⁰ Law Commission, Appendix D 'Comparative Consumer Law' 11, para.D.37; See generally Reinhard Zimmermann, 'Characteristic Aspects of German Legal Culture' in Mathias Reimann and Joachim Zekoll (ed), *Introduction to German law* (Kluwer Law International 2005); Reinhard Zimmermann, *The Law of Obligations: Roman Foundation of the Civilian Tradition* (Clarendon Press 1996).
¹¹ ibid. Law Commission para. D.39; Deutscher Bundestag, Drucksache 14/6040, 89;Peter Pott and Christian Twigg-Flesner (n 4) 134;Thomas Meiers, *Die Entwicklung und Reform der Sachmängelhaftung des Verkäufers beim Stückkauf* (Peter Lang GmbH 2010) 30.
¹² ibid.; See n 10.

position, since their rights expire after the moment of delivery, especially with regard to goods, which need to be examined more carefully to establish fault, paragraph 3 of article 3 of the Consumer Rights Directive provides a hierarchy of remedies which rely predominantly on the right to request a specific performance;[13] as a result, German law adopted the *performance* theory (*Erfüllungstheorie*) in section 437, as the seller is granted the opportunity to exercise a subsequent performance (*Nacherfüllung*) based on the right to cure the consumer for the delivery of a faulty good.[14] According to the newly adopted rules in line with the Directive, under the new order of the BGB a consumer has the right to request a repair or replacement from the seller under the first trier of consumer protection rights incorporated in section 439, unless it would is disproportionate or impossible;[15] for the purpose of choosing a remedy, the disproportionality test under article 3, paragraph 3 of the Directive has been implemented under section 439, number 3 in a two-fold fashion: relative and absolute disproportionality, which was already discussed briefly in the previous chapter. Furthermore, the right to reduction of price and termination of contract remain available to the consumer as a second trier of remedies.[16] As it seems, the intent of the BGB draft committee was to use the Directive as a tool for harmonization, clarification and modernization of the German law of obligations.

Section 3: From six months to two years – implementation of article 5 into the German legal order

The transposition effects of the Directive in Germany have had a particularly beneficial effect for consumers with regard to the right to lodge a claim.[17] In compari-

---

[13] Peter Rott, 'German Sales Law Two Years After the Implementation of Directive 1999/44/EC' (2004) 5 German Law Journal 238-239; The Directive (n 3) article 3, para. 3.

[14] Bürgerliches Gesetzbuch 2002 [hereinafter referred to as "BGB"] s 437; Section 433 refers to the obligation of the seller to deliver goods in conformity with a contract;See also Christian Zwarg, *Der Nacherfüllungsanspruch im BGB aus der Sicht eines verständigen* Käufers (Peter Lang GmbH 2010) 31; Gesa Kim Beckhaus, *Die Rechtsnatur der Erfüllung: Eine Kritische Betrachtung der Erfüllungstheorien unter besonderer Berücksichtigung der Schuldrechtsmodernisierung* (Mohr Siebeck 2012) 259; Volker Emmerich, *BGB-Schuldrecht Besonderer Teil* (C.F. Müller 2012) 18.

[15] ibid. BGB s 437, n 1 pursuant to s 439; Norbert Reich, 'Protection of Consumers' Economic Interests by EC Contract Law — Some Follow-up Remarks' (2006) 28 Syd LR 52; See generally Peter Rott, 'Minimum Harmonisation for the Completion of the Internal Market? The Example of Consumer Sales Law' (2003) 40 CML Rev 1107.

[16] ibid. BGB n.2 and 3; The Directive (n 3) article 3, para. 5.

[17] BGB (n 14) s 438.

son to the early rule on claims, which limited this right to only six months, after the incorporation of the two-year provision into section 438 of the German civil code the time to lodge a complaint has increased four times.[18] As a result, German consumers now enjoy a four times longer period for lodging claims. The drafters of the BGB found practical and economic reasons for including this limitation period in the new civil law code.

As a starting point, the expiry time for implementation of the Directive was 31 December 2001, which in practical terms means that from 1 January 2002 consumer groups would be empowered to seek damages, if the member state, in this case Germany, had failed to implement EU legislation on time.[19] Since the right to lodge a complaint for German consumers was substantially extended in time by the Consumer Rights Directive, it can be suggested that there was a very distinct chance that there might have been claims raised under the *Francovich* doctrine. Another issue that has to be taken into careful consideration is that even if the state implemented the Directive timely that would have had practical complications for the courts in the application of national law rules on equal footing with other EU law provisions, meaning there will be several parallel existing orders with regard to sale of goods in Germany.[20] On these grounds from an exclusively practical standpoint Germany had already had enough incentives to undertake immediate measures for the incorporation of the two-year limitation period.

Another argument in favour of the implementation of article 5 of the Consumer Rights Directive is that the longer limitation period would contribute greatly to the overall satisfaction of consumers, especially when they buy goods at the end of the season on a discount. According to the drafters of the new BGB, a person who buys ski equipment at the end of the winter season and does not use it throughout the summer

---

[18] Manfred Lange et al, *Sachversicherungen für private und gewerbliche Kunden Fach- und Führungskompetenz für die Assekuranz* (Verlag Versicherungswirtschaft 2014) 168; Marco Ardizzoni, *German Tax and Business Law* (Sweet & Maxwell 2005) 1035; Axel-Volkmar Jaeger and Götz-Sebastian Hök, *FIDIC - A Guide for Practitioners: A Guide for Practitioners* (Springer 2010) 312; Pierrick Le Goff, *Die Vertragsstrafe in internationalen Verträgen zur Errichtung von Industrieanlagen* (Tanea 2005) 172; See generally Hergen Scheck and Birgitt Scheck, *Wirtschaftliches Grundwissen: Für Naturwissenschaftler und Ingenieure* (JohnWiley & Sons 2012).
[19] Joined Cases C-6/90 and C-9/90 *Andrea Francovich v Italian Republic and Danila Bonifaci and Others and Italian Republic* [1991] ECR I-5375.
[20] See n 4.

under the older rule of six months can suffer from non-availability of remedies, if he realizes the good is not in conformity in December.[21] Furthermore, the two-year extended period would positively influence the second-hand car industry, since any faulty delivered tools can be repaired or replaced on time.[22] Nonetheless, in accordance with the basic notion that all goods differ in quality and durability, the German civil code has adopted different time rules depending on the type of good; for instance, stolen property can be claimed for 30 years, while under specific contractual obligations the period set for claims can be limited to one year.[23] As it appears, the newly adopted limitation period of two years is simple and straightforward in its wording and application. Although it has been modified by the German legislator under particular circumstances, there are strong arguments to consider it a legitimate restriction, since it is an indisputable fact that goods vary in quality and durability and this comprehensibly reflects the longer period for lodging claims. In the case of Germany the legislator's intent to implement article 5 of the Directive would be to boost consumer protection.

Section 4: Conclusion

Concluding, one cannot dispute that the implementation of articles 3 and 5 of the Directive into the domestic legal system of Germany has had a tremendous impact on the German law of obligations ever since. The linkage between the discussion on the ECJ case-law and the German law on consumer protection is not coincidental: both cases before the European court have dealt with inconsistencies of German norms with article 3 of the Directive, such as the two-fold disproportionality test and the financial burden on consumers for the usage of a faulty good. Moreover, the ambiguity of the wording of paragraph 3 of the same article, more precisely the phrase *'reasonable time'* in relation to the temporal scope of this provision causes legal confusion and raises questions about the simplicity of this provision, a fundamental principle of the Smart Regulation.[24] In addition, when this vague rule is applied in conjunction with the limitation period, there is little room for doubt that there can be clashes of serious degree, as the temporal unpredictability of another subsequent performance on behalf of

---

[21] Deutscher Bundestag (n 11) 228.
[22] ibid. 228-231.
[23] See n 17 n 1 under 1, 2 and 3.
[24] See n 13 The Directive; See also n 6.

the seller can bypass the effectiveness of a good rule of law, for instance the two-year warranty period. After giving a quick glance on the legal disturbances in German law assessed against the Consumer Rights Directive in the light of the Smart Regulation, the analysis on this legal system in the normative EU framework will follow later in this paper.[25]

---

[25] For a more detailed analysis, see Chapter 4.

Chapter 3: The English common law system and the legal transposition of articles 3 and 5 of the Consumer Rights Directive[1]

After having outlined how the Directive has been implemented in the legal framework of Germany as a classical civil law example, a contrast with the outcomes in the traditional common law order of England and Wales should follow. A short introduction of the characteristics of the common law regime and the rules on commercial disputes with regard to goods will be provided, identifying the legal position of the implemented norms under articles 3 and 5 of the Directive within the common law system. Throughout this chapter remarks will be made on the non-flexibility of the system to the supranational EU legal order. In conclusion, attention will be drawn to the legal tension between these two frameworks.

Section 1: Common law rules under the Sale of Goods Act[2]

It is relevant to outline that the English common law system is predominantly compensatory in nature;[3] such an outcome can be based on the historical development of the common law jurisdiction, where until the Judicature Acts 1873 and 1875 the role of the judges in the courts was only to award damages.[4] This well-established judicial practice is indicative of the fact that the English courts value highly common law traditions and tend to adhere to them. An example which would be appropriate in the spirit of this paper is the right to reject, which empowers the consumer to directly return the good, if faulty, to the seller after delivery and to terminate the contract.[5] The consumer can also refuse to pay for the good or demand a refund of the price.[6] Nonetheless, this right can be lost upon acceptance of the good in question, which, according to

---

[1] Directive 1999/44/EC of the European Parliament and of the Council of 25 May 1999 on certain aspects of the sale of consumer goods and associated guarantees [hereinafter referred as "The Directive"] OJ L 171.
[2] Sale of Goods Act 1979 [hereinafter referred as "SOGA"].
[3] Frank Schubert, *Introduction to Law and the Legal System* (Cengage Learning 2014) 224-226.
[4] Alisdair Gillespie, *The English Legal System* (Oxford University Press 2013) 12-13; John Wheeler, *Essentials of the English Legal System* (Pearson Education Limited 2006) 368-389; Mohamed Ramjohn *Beginning Equity and Trusts* (Routledge 2013) 16-17; Rebecca Huxley-Binns and Jacqueline Martin, *Unlocking the English Legal System* (Routledge 2014) 8-9.
[5] SOGA, s 35; See also Lucy Jones *Introduction to Business Law* (Oxford University Press 2013) 332; John MacLeod, *Consumer Sales Law* (Cavendish Publishing Limited 2002) 923.
[6] ibid. SOGA; Law Commission and Scottish Law Commission, *Consumer Remedies for Faulty Goods* (Law Com No 317, 2009), (SCOT Law Com No 216, 2009) para. 2.7.

the Act, is considered to have taken place on three occasions: when the buyer intimates with the seller or does something which is not consistent with the seller's ownership of the goods, or in the case where, *after a lapse of reasonable time*, the buyer keeps the goods without notifying the seller that the goods do not conform with the contract of sale.[7] This common law rule is a short-term remedy available to consumers under English law before any other remedy, as it combines an immediate rejection of a faulty good and a possibility of a refund.[8] Thus, the right to reject remains favorable in the common law order of England and Wales.

Section 2: Implementation of articles 3 and 5 of the Consumer Rights Directive in the Sale of Goods Act

Having in mind the fore-mentioned, the right to reject is in practice more significant in comparison to the remedial system of the EU Directive.[9] The Sale of Goods Act incorporated the newly adopted remedies under the Directive in a separate part – Part 5A, strategically isolated by the common law consumer rules.[10] As a result, this two-route approach has formed a complex procedural system, focused primarily on common law traditional judicial paths and using the new remedies under the Directive as an alternative means of decision-making.[11] Consumers have the right to choose a short-term remedy, such as the right to reject; however, they are also given the possibility of repair or replacement under the Directive. Legally speaking, the EU remedial system implemented into the English legal framework only complements the common law system; the right to reject prevails over the remedies proposed by the Directive.[12] The fact that there is no case-law on the new rules under Part 5A suggests that the implementation of article 3 of the Directive did not change the course of legal development in England and Wales.

---

[7] ibid. SOGA.
[8] Law Commission and Scottish Law Commission (n 6) para. 2.8.
[9] The Directive (n 1) article 3.
[10] SOGA (n 3) Part 5A; See also Norbert Reich, 'Protection of Consumer's Economic Interests by EC Contract Law' (2006) 28 Syd LR 37.
[11] See Annex I.
[12] Hector MacQueen, 'Europeanization of Contract Law' in Larry DiMatteo et al (ed), *Commercial Contract Law: Transatlantic Perspectives* (Cambridge University Press 2013) 555.

Unlike the new remedies adopted by the EU Directive, the two-year limitation period under article 5 has never been incorporated into the English legal order. The applicable rule with regard to faulty goods dates from 1980, when the prescribed period for bringing claims for lack of conformity with the good is six years.[13] The justification for this decision can be found in the difference in durability and quality of the goods, since some require more time to establish fault.[14] This is yet another clear example of the lack of flexibility of the common law order to adopt EU law rules; such an old limitation rule still applies.

Section 3: Conclusion

For the purposes of coherence, it would be essential to mention the most problematic areas in the legal relation between the English common law order and the Consumer Rights Directive. Although both the Law Commission and Scottish Law Commission have expressed their view that the law governing claims is already complicated enough[15] and Christian Twigg-Flesner's positively commented on the practical application of the right to reject within a prospective EU framework and the generally high consumer satisfaction rate,[16] the ambiguity of this rule raises serious concerns, in particular the temporal requirements for acceptance of a good.[17] The practical difficulties encountered in relation to these criteria can be observed by assessing the extensive case-law available on this matter, according to which *lapse of reasonable time* period varies from three months to over a year.[18] Lack of clarity in the wording of this provision is detrimental to the consumer and can constitute a violation with the simplicity principle of the Smart Regulation. Furthermore, having such a complicated remedial

---

[13] No guidelines given in the SOGA. The main principle of the Limitation Act 1980 in s 5, which sets out six years as a limitation period, remains. Nonetheless, it must be noted that the Law Commission has called for a reduction of this period to three years. For more detail, see Law Commission, *Limitation of Actions* (Law Com No. 270, 2001); See also Robert Bradgate and Fidelma White, *Commercial Law 2012: LPC Guide* (Oxford University Press 2012) 151; Denis J Keenan and Kenneth Smit, *Smith & Keenan's Law for Business* (Pearson Education Limited 2006) 290.
[14] Law Commission and Scottish Law Commission Report (n 6) 67 para. 6.61.
[15] Law Commission and Scottish Law Commission (n 6) para. 6.64.
[16] See generally Christian Twigg-Flesner, 'Fit for purpose? The proposals on sales' in Geraint Howells and Reiner Schulze (ed), *Modernising and Harmonising Consumer Contract Law* (2009).
[17] See n 5.
[18] See *Manifatture Tessile Laniera Wooltex v J B Ashley Limited* [1979] 2 Lloyd's Rep 28; *Bernstein v Pamson Motors (Golders Green) Limited* [1987] 2 All ER 220; *Truk (UK) Limited v Tokmakidis GmbH* [2000] 2 All ER (Comm) 594; *Fiat Auto Financial Services v Connelly* [2007] SLT (Sh Ct) 111.

system, as demonstrated by Annex I, with ambiguously worded rules can potentially lead to disproportional outcomes for the consumers, clashing with the proportionality rule under the European Commission initiative. Consequently, although consumers are awarded a longer period of six years for lodging claims for non-conformity of a good, the legal uncertainty as to when in time the consumer is considered to have accepted the good neutralizes the effectiveness of the extension. The following chapter will further elaborate on the legal inconsistencies between the common law order and the Consumer Rights Directive in the light of the Smart Regulation.

Chapter 4: Legal analysis of the implementation effects of articles 3 and 5 of the Consumer Rights Directive[1] into the domestic legal systems of Germany and England and Wales

After having demonstrated how Germany and England and Wales have adopted the new rules with regard to awarding relief and claims which the Directive underlines, this chapter of the paper concentrates on the legal effects the transposition of these provisions have within these two domestic legal orders as assessed in the light of the normative legal framework of the Smart Regulation.[2] As it has been indicated earlier in this paper, one of the legal struggles in Germany is the misinterpretation of the disproportionality test in article 3 of the Directive. The question which needs an urgent answer is whether its application in German courts has led to a violation with the principle of simplicity which the Smart Regulation promotes. Furthermore, another important observation would be the impact a potential ambiguous rule can have on a well-worded provision as the limitation period for claims under article 5 of the Directive in terms of proportionality. While Germany endeavors to organize its law of obligations in line with the principles of the EU, the English lawmakers have laid down reasons why England and Wales have been reluctant to any changes proposed by the Consumer Rights Directive, which will be critically discussed and assessed within the Smart Regulation framework. A closer insight will be provided with regard to the current applicable common law rules and the proposal of the English legislator for a Consumer Rights Bill, which aims to harmonize consumer law in England and Wales and whether, if voted in favour in the Parliament, it will be in the spirit of the Directive and the European traditions. In conclusion, a summary of the analysis will be provided designed to suggest an answer to the question whether or not the Directive, as applied in Germany and England and Wales, has complied with the principles of simplicity and proportionality within the normative framework of the Smart Regulation in order to ensure consumers a higher level of legal certainty.

---

[1] Directive 1999/44/EC of the European Parliament and of the Council of 25 May 1999 on certain aspects of the sale of consumer goods and associated guarantees [hereinafter referred to as "The Directive"] OJ L 171.

[2] IP/10/1296 (2010); See also COM (2010) 543 final; COM (2013) 685 final 1-5.

Section 1: Implementation effects of articles 3 and 5 of the Consumer Rights Directive on the German civil law system

As already discussed in the previous chapters, the transposition of the Directive has been used as an incentive to reform the whole regime of the German law of obligations, resulting in a newly drafted version of the Civil code.[3] Although the German legislators have implemented the Directive for the purpose of modernizing German law in line with EU principles,[4] article 3 concerning the new remedial hierarchy appears to have been misinterpreted and, consequently, misapplied into the German legal order. As a result, Germany has violated the EU values of simplicity and proportionality.

Subsection 1: Violation of article 3 of the Consumer Rights Directive and the principles of simplicity and proportionality of the Smart Regulation

A manifest example in support of this statement would be the wording and application of the disproportionality test under the Consumer Rights Directive as implemented in section 439 of the German Civil Code ("the BGB").[5] The German legislators from the beginning of the drafting process have expressed their view on the interpretation of this rule,[6] which later the European Court of Justice ("the ECJ") will reject, namely that the disproportionality test has two dimensions: relative and absolute disproportionality. The former refers to application of the test between the two available remedies under the first trier – repair and replacement, while the latter embraces the notion that even where one of the first trier remedies is available, it should not be granted in case its application would amount to great and excessive disproportionality to the determent of the seller.[7] Peter Pott and Christian Twigg-Flesner in an academic

---

[3] Stephen Weatherill, *EU Consumer Law and Policy* (Elgar Publishing Limited 2005) 134; Lucinda Miller, *The Emergence of EU Contract Law: Exploring Europeanization* (Oxford University Press 2011) 96.

[4] See generally Chapter 2, s 2; Norbert Reich, 'Protection of Consumers' Economic Interests by EC Contract Law — Some Follow-up Remarks' (2006) 28 Syd LR 52; Deutscher Bundestag , 166. Sitzung, 16213 (B).

[5] The Directive (n 1) article 3, para. 3; Bürgerliches Gesetzbuch 2002 [hereinafter referred as "BGB"] s 439, n. 3, sentence 2 and 3.

[6] Deutscher Bundestag, Drucksache 14/6040, 219-220.

[7] ibid.; See n 5; Hector MacQueen et al, 'Specific Performance and the Right to Cure' in Gerhard Dannemann and Stefan Vogenauer (ed), *The Common European Sales Law in Context: Interactions with English and German law* (Oxford University Press 2013) 627-628; Michael Jaensch, *Grundzüge des Bürgerlichen Rechts: mit 63 Fällen und Lösungen* (C.F. Müller 2012) 210.

contribution have discussed and supported this line of reasoning of the Bundestag.[8] They claimed that the test in itself is ambiguous as it has to be clarified to which trier of remedies it applies – either to repair and replacement only or between the two triers under article 3 of the Directive.[9] As both academics concluded that the relative disproportionality test is illogical, because there cannot be a situation where both remedies are found either disproportionate or impossible, they arrived at the conclusion that at least one remedy should be made available before moving to the second trier of remedies.[10] Therefore, Pott and Twigg-Flesner seem to have favoured the two-fold interpretation of the disproportionality test. Nonetheless, after careful consideration, few would deny the fact that having such a double standard can cause legal confusion. The absolute disproportionality interpretation is a slippery slope, which can contradict with the very idea of the Directive, to improve the quality and level of consumer protection.[11] The case of *Gebr. Weber/Ingrid Putz* is indicative of this fact.[12] Although Pott and Twigg-Flesner support the notion that there should be at least one remedy available under the first trier before moving to reduction of price and termination of contract, the above-mentioned case of the European Court of Justice ("the ECJ") proves that absolute proportionality constitutes a safeguard for the seller, leaving the consumer without a remedy; the court rejected such an interpretation of the rule, arguing that this line of reasoning would deprive the consumer of a short-term remedy.[13] Moreover, this fact would lead to disproportionate outcomes to the detriment of the consumer, which conflicts directly with the aim of the Directive to provide a high level of consumer protection.[14] The ECJ rules that the German courts are in violation with the standards imposed by the Consumer Rights Directive and favoured the relative disproportionality test only between

---

[8] Peter Pott and Christian Twigg-Flesner, 'No Closer to Harmonisation? The Implementation of Directive 1999/44/EC into English and German Law Three Years On' in Geraint Howells et al (ed), *The Yearbook of Consumer Law 2007* (Publisher 2007).
[9] ibid. 141.
[10] ibid. 142.
[11] The Directive (n 1) recital 1.
[12] Joined Cases C-65/09 and C-97/09 *Gebr.Weber GmbH v Jürgen Wittmer, and Ingrid Putz v Medianess Electronics GmbH* [hereinafter referred as "Gebr. Weber"] [2011] ECR I-5257.
[13] ibid. 65.
[14] ibid.

repair and replacement,[15] according to which the consumer should be granted a remedy if it is available and not impossible at expense of the seller.[16]

This case has demonstrated that the German legislator has not adopted the rule on disproportionality correctly. A two-fold vague test with no guidelines what constitutes such excessive disproportionality to the seller can be applied against the consumer, which is an example of a violation with the simplicity principle in the framework of the Smart Regulation. Vagueness of the rule giving access to a collection of remedies to the consumer in fact has left them without a remedy, as it was the case in *Gebr.Weber/Ingrid Putz*. The effect of having no available, effective remedy could be described as causing disproportionate outcome to the consumer, which also conflicts with the principle of proportionality. If a rule contradicts with its main idea, then this provision is not proportionate in its effect. Consequently, section 439 of the German civil code has violated the principle of simplicity and proportionality in applying article 3 of the Consumer Rights Directive.

The other landmark decision of the ECJ in relation to article 3 of the Directive – the popular *Quelle AG* case, demonstrates that German law has failed to incorporate correctly this provision of the Directive. The German legislators have implemented article 3 in section 439 while drafting the new civil code, stating that upon termination of the contract, the buyer is expected to cover for the usage of the good.[17] The court in *Quelle AG* ruled that, based on the main principle of consumer protection laid down under article 3, paragraph 1, that the seller should bear all consequences of his failure to deliver a non-faulty good, the consumer should not pay for the usage of a faulty good.[18] In this case, the German government claimed that under recital 15 the drafters had the

---

[15] Christian Twigg-Flesner, *The Europeanisation of Contract Law: Current Controversies in Law* (Routledge 2013) 109.
[16] Gebr. Weber (n 12) 68.
[17] BGB (n 5) s 439, n 4 pursuant to s 346, n 1 and 3; Deutscher Bundestag, Drucksache 14-6857, 25, para. 88.
[18] Case C-404/06 *Quelle AG v Bundesverband der Verbraucherzentralen und Verbraucherverbände* [hereinafter referred as "Quelle AG"] [2008] ECR I-2685 paras. 26-27 and 43; See also Stephen Weatherhill, 'Consumer Policy' in Paul P. Craig and Gráinne De Búrca (ed), *The Evolution of EU law* (Oxford University Press 2011) 859; Christian Twigg-Flesner (n 15) 108; Stephen Weatherhill, *EU Consumer Law and Policy* (Eldar Publishing Limited 2013) 164; Stephen Weatherhill, 'Interpretation of the Directives: The Role of the Court' in Arthur Hartkamp et al (ed), *Towards a European Civil Code* (Kluwer Law International 2011) 194; Gabriël Moens and John Trone, *Commercial Law of the European Union* (Springer 2010) 323.

option to include such a rule for reimbursement; the court disagreed stating that the *ratio* behind is that the seller should reimburse the consumer the selling price of the good pursuant to article 3, paragraph 5 of the Directive and that this recital cannot be otherwise interpreted.[19]

One can conclude from the ruling in this case that German law, in particular section 439 in conjunction with section 346 of the BGB, in applying article 3 of the Directive has not respected the principle of proportionality promoted by the Smart Regulation, because it imposed financial burden to the consumer for the usage of a faulty good, which acts contrary to the aim of the Directive being high protection for consumers.

Subsection 2: Article 5 of the Consumer Rights Directive and its adherence to the principles of simplicity and proportionality under the Smart Regulation

Whereas there have been violations with regard to article 3 and the newly adopted remedial system, the imposed two-year limitation period in Germany constitutes a beneficial extension of the earlier rule of six months.[20] The longer period for claims could contribute greatly to the overall satisfaction of consumers, especially when they buy second-hand goods or discounted goods.[21] Furthermore, the two-year extended period would positively influence the second-hand car industry, since any faulty delivered tools can be repaired or replaced on time.[22] Nonetheless, on the ground that all goods differ in quality and durability, the German civil code has adopted different time rules depending on the type of good; for instance, stolen property can be claimed for 30 years, while under specific contractual obligations the period set for claims can be limited to one year.[23] This categorization on behalf of the German legislators seems

---

[19] ibid. Quelle AG paras. 37-39.
[20] The Directive (n 1) article 5; BGB (n 5) s 438; See Chapter 2; Mauro Bussani and Franz Werro, *European private law* (Stämpfli Publishers 2001) 281; Dennis Campbell, *Remedies for International Sellers of Goods [2009] – II* (Yorkhill Law Publishing 2009) 12; Bastiaan van Zelst, *The Politics of European Sales Law: A Legal-political Inquiry Into the the drafting of the Uniform Commercial Code, the Vienna Sales Convention, the Dutch Civil Code and the European Consumer Sales Directive in the context of the Europeanisation of contract law* (Kluwer Law International 2008) 209.
[21] Deutscher Bundestag (n 6) 228.
[22] ibid.
[23] BGB (n 5) n 1 under 1, 2 and 3.

legitimate and in line with the spirit of the Directive as a whole.[24] For this reason, it appears to be a reasonable, legitimate and simply-worded rule.

Consequently, in the case of Germany the extended period for claims from six months to two years and its further differentiation boosts consumer protection, meets the requirements of simplicity of the law promoted by the Smart Regulation and is directly proportional to the aims of the Directive.

Subsection 3: Interdependence of articles 3 and 5 of the Consumer Rights Directive

As it has been demonstrated above, the interrelation between simplicity and proportionality is vital for the coherent application of a provision. The two-year warranty period under article 5 is indeed a success in the context of the German law of obligations. Albeit simple from the outset, the application of this provision faces practical difficulties, which flow from the legal lack of clarity of the rule governing remedies under article 3. Since consumers have to wait '*reasonable* time' for a subsequent performance on behalf of the seller,[25] practically claims are lodged in a deadlock position. Although the consumer has exercised his right to claim a repair or delivery of a new good in conformity with the contract, in practice this procedure might take an indefinite period of time, which undermines the simplicity and proportionality of the two-year limitation period. This is an example of how legal ambiguity and irregularities can neutralize the positive effect of a well-worded and simplified procedural provision. Furthermore, an unidentified temporal scope of the rule of subsequent performance could place the consumer in a very disadvantageous position waiting for another repair or replacement for indefinite time, which practically deprives them from taking any other action against the seller, for instance termination of contract or reduction of price. A consumer who requested additional performance under the first trier of remedies has to provide the seller with *reasonable* time.[26]

This is a demonstration that the Directive in practice is a chain of rules – if one provision does not comply with the principle of simplicity and causes disproportionate

---

[24] The Directive (n 1) article 8, para. 2.
[25] See n 5 paras.3 and 5.
[26] See n 25.

results, another provision pursuant to it, albeit simple in its wording and beneficial in its application, can suffer from ineffectiveness. In the present case, the vagueness of section 439 of the German civil code implementing article 3 of the Directive could place the straight-forward rule of the two-year warranty period in section 438 in a deadlock position, violating the principles of simplicity and proportionality under the Smart Regulation.

Subsection 4: Conclusion

It can be summarized that, as the early academic discussions on the transposition effects of the Consumer Rights Directive in Germany by Pott and Twigg-Flesner and the explanations of the law made by the drafters of the new BGB have indicated, Germany has misinterpreted and misapplied article 3 and 5. As a result, this has led to breaches with EU law before the ECJ and the principles of simplicity and proportionality within the framework of the Smart Regulation. Thus, consumers suffer from legal confusion and uncertainty as a consequence of the incorrect interpretation of these provisions of the Directive.

Section 2: Implementation effects of articles 3 and 5 of the Consumer Rights Directive within the English common law order

In the previous chapter it has been mentioned that the common law regime in England and Wales is reluctant to the changes imposed by the Consumer Rights Directive. The provisions the Directive have been included in a separate part of the Sale of Goods Act 1979 ("SOGA")[27], isolated from the applicable common law rules. The Law Commission and the Scottish law Commission in their report from 2009 elaborated on their decision to adhere to the well-established traditions of common law and the problems English courts might encounter in the application of the rules under the Directive.

---

[27] Sale of Goods Act 1979 [hereinafter referred as "SOGA"] Part 5A; Jill Poole, *Textbook on Contract Law* (Oxford University Press 2014) 297.

Subsection 1: Potential issues with article 3 of the Consumer Rights Directive

The remedies under article 3 of the Directive as transposed in the SOGA are of supplementary character to the primary common law remedy – the right to refuse.[28] Consumers do have the right to demand repair or replacement; however, as a consequence, they lose the right to reject the good, as the seller should be given a reasonable amount of time to either deliver or repair the faulty good.[29] The Law Commission and the Scottish law Commission expressed their concerns about a potential prevalence of the strict hierarchy of remedies as proposed by the Directive and potential effects on the common law order.

In the first place, the characteristics of the common law system, being compensatory in nature,[30] presuppose that award of damages will be the most frequently awarded relief. This is indicative of the fact why the right to refuse still plays a central role in the remedial system in England and Wales; this practice is deeply rooted in the principle of consumer confidence, since the type of remedy is immediate, straightforward and, for these reasons, preferred by a good number of consumers, according to the latest investigations by the Law Commissions.[31] Furthermore, it promotes trust in the consumer-seller relationship and grants consumers a first-hand remedy of immediate effect.[32] The greater part of consumers interviewed related their willingness to buy goods with the possibility to return the good directly in case it is faulty.[33] In a nutshell, adherence to the common law traditions would avoid complications of practical importance for the English courts.

In the second place, as the Law Commission and the Scottish Law Commission stated in their report, it would be a real danger for English consumers to be trapped in a

---

[28] ibid. SOGA s 35; See also Hector MacQueen et al (n 7) 617.
[29] ibid. SOGA s 52; See also Jill Poole (n 35); Denis Keenan and Kenneth Smith, *Smith & Keenan's Law for Business* (Longman 2006) 290; Mirghasem Jafarzadeh, 'Buyer's Right to Specific Performance' in Michael Maggi (ed), *Review of the Convention on Contracts for the International Sale of Goods (CISG) 2002-2003* (Kluwer Law International 2004) 159-160.
[30] See Chapter 3.
[31] Law Commission and Scottish Law Commission, *Consumer Remedies for Faulty Goods* (Law Com No 317, 2009), (Scot Law Com No 216, 2009) 21-24.
[32] ibid. 21 on the Office of Fair Trading reasoning.
[33] Law Commission and Scottish Law Commission, *Consumer Remedies For Faulty Goods: A Joint Consultation Paper* (Law Com CP No 188, 2009), (Scot Law Com DP No 139, 2009) 136.

cycle of failed repairs and replacements.[34] Without the right to reject as a short-term relief, the consumer will be bound to the vague and ambiguous rule of *'reasonable time'* for execution of a subsequent performance under article 3, paragraph 3 of the Directive and the lack of reference to any criteria with regard to the temporal scope of this provision.[35] Such outcomes would heavily jeopardize the well-established principle of maintaining consumer confidence in England and Wales;[36] on this ground, the Commission report suggests that there should be a limitation of failed attempts for either repair or replacement, because it would at the very least provide a numerical reflection of legal certainty for consumers.[37] From all reasons stated, it can be summarized that the Law Commission and the Scottish Law Commission are reluctant to incorporate the remedial hierarchy under the Directive, since it lacks clarity, which inevitably means that article 3 as applied in English law would undermine the principle of simplicity promoted by the Smart Regulation.

A final argument for isolating the remedies under the Consumer Rights Directive lies on a financial ground. Although the seller bears responsibility for covering expenses for specific performance, for instance delivery costs, the days off work the consumer has to take in order to accept the delivery or to welcome the repair team, the telephone calls to arrange an appointment, the lack of temporary substitution of the good in question and the indefinite period of waiting time for a repair or replacement (*'reasonable time'*) seem to be legitimate reasons to critically assess the proportionality of the rule of subsequent performance under article 3, paragraph 3.[38] It appears to be a burdensome means for ordinary people of acquiring an adequate remedy *'free of charge'*.[39]

Thus, it can be maintained that the application of article 3 into the common law regime of England and Wales would disregard the principle of simplicity embedded in the Smart Regulation and the consequences of such legal inconsistency could be

---

[34] Law Commission and Scottish Law Commission (n 31) 60-61.
[35] ibid. 61-62.
[36] Law Commission, *Impact Assessment of Consumer Remedies for Faulty Goods* paras. 34-35.
[37] Law Commission and Scottish Law Commission (n 31) 61 paras. 6.20-6.21.
[38] The Office of Fair Trading (OFT), 'Consumer Detriment: Assessing the frequency and impact of consumer problems with goods and services' (2008) OFT 992, 22-26.
[39] The Directive (n 1) article 3, paras.2 and 3.

observed in disproportionate outcomes for consumers, further breaching the principle of proportionality.

Subsection 2: Primary common law rule of the six-year limitation period

With regard to article 5 and the two-year limitation period for lodging claims, which according to the Directive lasts two years, the applicable common law norm is six years.[40] The English common law system has not adopted the shorter period for complaints on the grounds that some faults require more time to be discovered, depending on the quality, nature and type of the good.[41] It has been further suggested that the existing time restrictions for lodging claims are already complicated enough.[42] Moreover, the Faculty of Advocates considered that it would be misleading for consumers into thinking that the default time frames apply as usual, only to realize that there is a much shorter period of time applicable.[43] Thus, multiple time limits only would add to the complexity of the law,[44] which will contradict the principle of simplicity of the Smart Regulation.

Another argument in favour of keeping the standard limitation period for claims in England and Wales can be found in the warranty period for more durable and long-lasting goods, such as cars. In such situations more time will be needed for faults to occur. If consumers would be time-barred in such cases, it would, on the one hand, be unfair, thus, causing disproportionate outcomes for the consumer who would not have access to a remedy, and it would discourage manufacturers, on the other, to maintain a high level of quality of the goods they produce.[45] In this sense, the two-year limitation period would lack proportionality towards both parties.

It can be concluded that within the common law system of England and Wales the two-year warranty period prescribed by the Consumer Rights Directive would add

---

[40] Limitation Act 1980 s 5; The Law Commission proposed a reduction of this period to from six to three years. For a more detailed discussion, see Law Commission, *Limitation of Actions* (Law Com No 270, 2001).
[41] Law Commission and Scottish Law Commission Report (n 31) 67 para. 6.61.
[42] ibid. 68 para. 6.63.
[43] ibid.
[44] ibid. para. 6.64 on the opinion of the City of London Law Society.
[45] ibid. on the Consumer Focus suggestion.

to a more complex system of law which lacks simplicity and would, additionally, be burdensome to the consumer and, thus, would lack proportionality within the normative framework of the Smart Regulation.

Subsection 3: Conclusion

It can be concluded that the common law system in England and Wales has not embraced fully the newly proposed remedial system under article 3 and has not implemented at all the shorter period for lodging claims under article 5 of the Directive. According to the Law Commission and Scottish Law Commission, there were fears that their transposition would lead to legal complications and tension and discourage consumer trust, which assessed within the Smart Regulation framework, would breach the principles of proportionality and simplicity.

Section 3: Summary

In conclusion, very few would deny the fact that the Consumer Rights Directive as applied in Germany, on the one hand, violates both the principles of simplicity and proportionality within the framework of the Smart Regulation; thus, the Directive did not contribute to a higher level of legal certainty for consumers in the German case. Since its provisions have been misinterpreted, wrongly implemented and, consequently, misapplied, the European Court of Justice ruled on two major occasions – *Quelle AG* and *Gebr. Weber/Ingrid Putz*, that the German authorities are at fault in the application of the Directive. The Directive's provisions in England and Wales, on the other, have been partially implemented and incorporated as additional remedies available in a complex dual remedial system,[46] for the fear of complicating the common law order additionally, leading to a violation with the principles under the Smart Regulation.

---

[46] See Annex I.

Concluding remarks

Having assessed the implications of the Consumer Rights Directive[1] within the domestic legal orders of Germany and England and Wales against the principles of simplicity and proportionality promoted by the Smart Regulation initiative of the European Commission, few would deny the fact that the law on consumer protection needs to be urgently consolidated and simplified in order to serve as a means to provide legal certainty. As a result, consumers would enjoy more proportionate and effective outcomes due to a more harmonized and uniform practice of the domestic legal mechanisms. For these reasons, a list of prospective legal improvements in the domestic legal orders of Germany and England and Wales will be provided in conclusion as well as recommendations for development on European level with regard to the Consumer Rights Directive in order to ensure a smooth, more comprehensive and simplified system in line with the principles of the Smart Regulation.

Germany

Although the German authorities have incorporated straightforwardly article 3 of the Consumer Rights Directive, it has been observed in the previous chapter that their implementation has led to violations with the principles of simplicity and proportionality under the Smart Regulation initiative. In order to remove these obstacles and ensure a higher level of consumer protection in Germany, the legislator has to undertake amendments in the German civil code, so that German law applies in line with the spirit of the Directive.

Recommendation 1: Implementation of a strict rule prohibiting additional charge on the consumer

After the landmark case for the German law of obligations – *Quelle AG*,[2] the only legislative change which has been undertaken by the legislator was the adoption of a

---

[1] Directive 1999/44/EC of the European Parliament and of the Council of 25 May 1999 on certain aspects of the sale of consumer goods and associated guarantees [hereinafter referred as "The Directive"] OJ L 171.
[2] Case C-404/06 *Quelle AG v Bundesverband der Verbraucherzentralen und Verbraucherverbände* [hereinafter referred as "Quelle AG"] [2008] ECR I-2685.

provision defining the scope of the notion 'defective good';[3] before the judgment of the European Court of Justice what constitutes a defect was not specifically prescribed by law. Although this legislative step could be considered to be of crucial importance for further rulings ensuring a higher level of consumer protection, the obligation under section 439, number 4 of the BGB for consumers to cover for the expenses for the usage of a faulty good, which has been rebutted by the court in *Quelle AG*, has not been repealed by the German authorities yet.[4] This line of reasoning by the German government has been rejected strongly by the ECJ; however, no further action has been undertaken. According to the members of the German parliament (*Bundestag*), the legislative authorities (*Bundesrat*) have to regulate this matter more concisely, drafting a specific provision, since this would enhance legal certainty for consumers and would clarify and unify legal rules in relation to consumer protection.[5] Moreover, a mere consistent interpretation in conformity with the reasoning of the ECJ would not be enough to achieve this goal.[6] Thus, the need for implementation of this particular legal rule is incumbent for establishing a coherent system of remedies in line with the spirit of the Smart Regulation initiative and the principles of simplicity and proportionality.

Recommendation 2: Deletion of the absolute disproportionality limb of the disproportionality test

The most important conclusion of the *Gebr.Weber/Ingrid Putz*[7] case is the prevalence the court gave to the relative disproportionality test. Nonetheless, the twofold test has not yet been changed and can be found in the BGB under section 439, number 3. Leaving this provision as part of the enforceable body of rules in the German legal order would lead to a failure on behalf of Germany to fulfill its obligations towards the European Union after having been condemned for incorrect application of the Consumer Rights Directive. Consistent interpretation of this section with article 3 of the Directive would not be sufficient, since it would be *contra legem*; without any specific reference to what constitutes 'excessive disproportionality to the detriment of

---

[3] Bürgerliches Gesetzbuch 2002 [hereinafter referred as "BGB"] s 434.
[4] ibid. s 439 , n 3.
[5] Deutscher Bundestag, Drucksache 17/12637, 92-93 para. 15.
[6] ibid.
[7] Joined Cases C-65/09 and C-97/09 *Gebr.Weber GmbH v Jürgen Wittmer, and Ingrid Putz v Medianess Electronics GmbH* [hereinafter referred to as "Gebr. Weber"] [2011] ECR I-5257.

the seller' would provide them with additional safeguards, which is contrary to the aims of the Directive to ensure protection for consumers as a weaker party in a commercial dispute. For this reason, an urgent compromise as to the alteration of this provision under the BGB is needed in order to comply with the judgment *Gebr.Weber/Ingrid Putz*. Thus, number 3 of section 439 has to be deleted from the BGB. Otherwise, sellers would continue to enjoy a 'safe heaven' under German law, which would further breach the principle of proportionality under the Smart Regulation.

Consequently, Germany should invest efforts in ensuring a higher level of consumer protection, since apart from the implemented definition for 'defective good', there is urgent need for legislative changes in the German civil code in order to combat legal uncertainty caused by the misapplication of the Directive's provisions. Furthermore, consistent judicial practice is not anymore considered enough to avoid disproportionate outcomes for the buyer, according to the Bundestag. Thus, parliamentary debates must continue on essential legal points and be more productive in the near future for the purpose of unifying the German legal system with EU law principles, such as simplicity and proportionality. Nonetheless, one has to take into account the fact that legislative amendments are likely to be a time-consuming process, which needs consensus and careful consideration. Unsurprisingly, the German authorities, three years after the ruling of *Gebr. Weber/Ingrid Putz*, have not yet reached a conclusion as to how to implement the changes imposed by the ECJ.

England and Wales

Unlike Germany, the English common law system has implemented article 3 only as an alternative route to seek relief, supplementary to the primary rule on the right to reject;[8] the Law Commission and the Scottish Law Commission outlined reasons why consumer would prefer the right to directly return the good to the seller, if faulty.[9] It has been, therefore, also included as a primary means to award remedies under the newly proposed Consumer Rights Bill 2014 before the House of Lords.[10] Although it has been suggested that the right to reject should serve only as a short-term remedy, case-law has

---

[8] Sale of Goods Act 1979 [hereinafter referred as "SOGA"] Part 5A.
[9] Law Commission and Scottish Law Commission, *Consumer Remedies For Faulty Goods: A Joint Consultation Paper* (Law Com CP No 188, 2009), (Scot Law Com DP No 139, 2009) 136.
[10] Consumer Rights Bill HC Bill (2013-14) [161] [hereinafter referred as "The Bill"], cl. 21, para. 1.

proved that the temporal scope of this norm is undefined and subject to broad interpretation by the English courts. As a result, a possible time restriction of the application of this right is necessary in order to comply with the principles of simplicity and proportionality under the Smart Regulation.

Recommendation 1: Categorization of the right to reject

The right to reject is designed to provide immediate, short-term relief to consumers in England and Wales. However, this right can be waived, if '*a lapse of reasonable time*' has passed and the consumer did not inform the seller of any fault established.[11] The main issue with this norm is that it suffers from unpredictability, since case-law has proven it is extremely hard to determine what constitutes a reasonable time period for accepting a good. The Law Commission and the Scottish Law Commission have proposed a 30-day period for returning a good, which has been later implemented in the Consumer Rights Bill 2014.[12] However, even the drafters of the Bill agreed that such a rigid test cannot be applied towards all goods;[13] determinants for its application are the type and the nature of the good, the circumstances involved in the purchase of the good, etc. As a result, the imposition of the 30-day period for lodging claims would be subject to interpretation on a case-by-case basis, which would not improve much the level of consumer protection and legal certainty for consumers. For this reason, it would be a good suggestion for the English common law system to adopt a more categorized approach towards this issue. For instance, the English authorities can use the German example with regard to the two-year limitation period:[14] the rule under article 5 of the Directive has been further categorized depending on the nature and the type of the good, since the Directive itself provides for such an opportunity to impose stringent rules with regard to the limitation period on national level.[15] Thus, the right to reject can be further divided into separate categories according to established court rulings, for example a category for new goods, as in the *Bernstein v Pamson Motors (Golders Green) Limited*

---

[11] SOGA (n 8) s 35.
[12] Law Commission and Scottish Law Commission, *Consumer Remedies for Faulty Goods* (Law Com No 317, 2009), (Scot Law Com No 216, 2009) 30; See n 10.
[13] The Draft 'Consumer Rights Bill' HC Bill (2013-2014) [697-I] [hereinafter referred to as "The Draft"] 16-17.
[14] BGB (n 3) s 438.
[15] The Directive (n 1) article 8, para. 2.

case,[16] second-hand goods or new goods which, after establishment of fault, have undergone several failed repairs; *Fiat Auto Financial Services v Connelly*[17] is a case in point. Additionally, there can be an exception provided, according to which these time frames can be extended in case of fraudulent behavior, such as hiding information on faults on the good, as in *Clegg v Andersson T/A Nordic Marine*.[18] Such fragmentation of the rule would bring more clarity with regard to its application and would boost consumer trust in England and Wales and, thus, legal certainty for consumers; at the same time, such a wording would be considered in line with the principle of simplicity and proportionality under the Smart Regulation.

As a result, the clause on the 30-day period under the proposed Consumer Rights Bill 2014 and the 'lapse of reasonable time' requirement for acceptance of a good should be deleted and replaced by a categorization of the right to reject. Nonetheless, one has to take into careful consideration the nature of the common law system, primarily its rigidity to new rules and the likelihood to implement new time restrictions for lodging claims. It has been maintained that multiple time limitations would only add to the complexity of the law, thus, infringing the principle of simplicity under the Smart Regulation initiative and leading to a lower level of consumer confidence in the judicial system. Thus, to avoid such confusion, the English legislator has to be cautious with regard to the wording of provisions and, hence, being more straight-forward in relation to each category than opaque and questionable. In addition, references to the principles of simplicity and proportionality under the Smart Regulation could be used as a self-correction tool for the new norms in order to bring English common law traditions in line with the spirit of the European order.

Directive 1999/44/EC

As it has been demonstrated, the application of article 3 of the Directive within the domestic orders of Germany and England and Wales assessed against the principles of simplicity and proportionality under the Smart Regulation initiative has been inconsistent; it identified specific areas of law which need to be repealed in order to reach

---

[16] *Bernstein v Pamson Motors (Golders Green) Limited* [1987] 2 All ER 220.
[17] *Fiat Auto Financial Services v Connelly* [2007] SLT (Sh Ct) 111.
[18] *Clegg v Andersson T/A Nordic Marine* [2003] EWCA Civ 320; [2003] 1 All ER (Comm) 721.

compliance with the European tradition. However, few would dispute the fact that the very source of these legal gaps lies with legal ambiguity within the wording of the Consumer Rights Directive itself. The problems encountered on national level, in this sense, envisage the legal lacunas embedded in the provisions of the Directive. For this reason, a reference should be made in order to connect the struggles in national courts with regard to the implementation of the Directive and its possible improvements, which would lead to a more simplified and comprehensive system for the benefit of the consumer as a whole.

Recommendation 1: Explicit reference to the relative disproportionality test in article 3, paragraph 3 of the Directive

As illustrated in the German example, in *Gebr. Weber/Ingrid Putz* case it has been ruled that prevalence has to be given to the relative disproportionality test under article 3.[19] Nonetheless, paragraph 3 is not exhaustive on this matter. The fact that it provides an opportunity to reconsider the gravity of damage caused by the seller and to link it to the costs imposed so that they are not disproportionate to the seller in fact leave the impression that the notion of absolute disproportionality has been implied within the article of the Directive in the first place. Thus, the wording of article 3 leaves room for interpretation of the disproportionality test, as the German authorities approached it in the case before the ECJ. For this reason, it would be a good suggestion to alter this paragraph and adopt the line of interpretation promoted by the court in the *Gebr.Weber/Ingrid Putz* case, namely the relative disproportionality approach. As a result, repair and replacement would be weighed against each other and disproportionality would be established only for the purposes of ensuring a higher quality of consumer satisfaction in cases where the other available remedy would contribute more in comparison to the other. For instance, in case of a fault in a part of a one year and a half old washing machine, such as the engine, consumers would prefer to have a brand new machine instead of repairing this specific part; the weighing effect a repair in this case can have on consumer satisfaction and a replacement with a new and never used washing machine seems to be self-evident, as most consumers would prefer rather a new product than a used one. Thus, disproportionality has to be assessed against the

---

[19] Gebr. Weber (n 7) 68.

principle of consumer satisfaction, wording this provision with a manifest adherence to the relative disproportionality approach taken by the ECJ, respecting simplicity and proportionality.

Recommendation 2: Number of repairs/replacements under the first trier of article 3, paragraph 3 of the Directive

As the Law Commission and the Scottish Law Commission indicated, the lack of a numerical reflection as to how many repairs or replacements have to take place before reconsidering reduction of price and termination of contract for adequate measures.[20] This could be a point of improvement within the wording of the Directive. It can be stated in the disproportionality test that when the seller chooses between a repair and replacement basing their decision on the consumer satisfaction rule, a number of repairs or replacements have to take place before exhausting the first trier of remedies. For example, there should be one failed repair or replacement before a request on reduction of price and termination of contract follows. In the abovementioned case, only one unsuccessful replacement should be enough for consumers to be granted access to the second trier of remedies.[21] Otherwise, the well-established principle of consumer confidence and trust in the seller responsible for delivering non-faulty goods will be undermined. As a result, article 3 under paragraph 3 has to provide consumers with a number of failed repairs or replacements, preceding reduction of price and termination of contract in order to comply with the principles of simplicity and proportionality under the Smart Regulation. It cannot be denied that a prescription of a specific number of performances would make the provision more rigid; nonetheless, it would promote consumer trust, since consumers would be more likely to rely on a straight-forward, limiting rule than on a vague case-by-case determination of the norms.

Recommendation 3: The right to reject as a transitory means to justice

According to the English common law regime, the right to reject is the primary short-term remedy which is applicable in consumer disputes, underlying its immediacy. However, this right is not incorporated under the Consumer Rights Directive remedial scheme. Since the Law Commission and the Scottish Law Commission argue that it

---

[20] Law Commission and Scottish Law Commission (n 12) 61 paras. 6.20-6.21.
[21] ibid. 65.

boost consumer confidence and strengthen the consumer-seller relationship of trust, leading to English consumers being more willing to purchase more if they are awarded the right to reject, implies that its overall effectiveness as a tool to seek relief should not be undermined.[22] Moreover, according to an investigation assessing European jurisdictions, at least nine of the member states in the European Union have implemented the right to reject.[23] Furthermore, before the adoption of the Consumer Rights Directive, this principle has been applicable in many other member states, according to the Green Paper on Guarantees for Consumer Goods and After-sales Services issued by the European Commission, including Germany and UK.[24] Following this line of reasoning, one can reach the conclusion that the right to reject would be legitimately incorporated into the European legal framework. A question which rises is under what circumstances. For a smoother transition between the first trier and the second trier of remedies it would be a good suggestion to include the right to reject. Thus, if, applying the disproportionality test, a repair would be more beneficial and appropriate in the given case and the seller performs subsequently, but the performance fails, the consumer should be awarded with the right to return the good directly and demand full refund. If not, they may proceed to the second trier. Such a procedure would satisfy both European standards and national traditions, since it promotes a new remedial system with a strict hierarchy; nonetheless, at the same time, the importance of member states traditional practices is not undermined and the legal relationship between the two is kept intact. Nevertheless, the biggest challenge before the European legislator would be to implement this right in a uniform manner, since this right had an application of one kind in Germany before for instance and has yet an application of another in England and Wales. Careful consideration has to be taken also when temporally restricting the right to reject, since it has to directly follow one (or more, depending on the number) failed repair or replacement and, for this reason, action should be taken immediately after fault has been established and the seller has been contacted. The term immediately, nonetheless, might trigger hot legal discussions.

---

[22] ibid. 21 on the Office of Fair Trading reasoning; See also n 9.
[23] ibid. 25.
[24] 'Green Paper on Guarantees for Consumer Goods and After-sales Services' COM (1993) 509 final.

For all of the above-mentioned reasons, an implementation of the right to reject into the Consumer Rights Directive framework would be a compromise between the European legal order and the legal traditions of member states, since it has been deeply rooted as a norm in consumer law not only in England and Wales, but also in a good number of Westernized civil law systems. Hence, its incorporation of the Directive would follow naturally.

Conclusion

It is recommendable that the EU Commission takes into account the current legal developments in Germany and England and Wales in case a fitness check is undertaken as to reconsider the effectiveness of the Directive as a whole. The legal lacunas in the domestic systems of member states with regard to the application of provisions under the Directive are a clear indication that a more uniform and simplified approach on a supranational level towards this field of law is urgently needed. Moreover, a clear, consolidated and straight-forward centralized regime would unify the traditions of member states, which would, thus, lead to a higher level of consumer protection. Furthermore, the parliamentary discussions and legislative suggestions also deserve to be paid due regard in order to align potentially adopted EU norms and national law rules in order to avoid legal inconsistency of both interpretation and application of the law, since the interdependence of EU and national legal orders is of crucial importance, as demonstrated in this legal analysis. Additionally, potential interest groups, such as legal consultants, bureaus for protection of consumers, representatives of small and medium enterprises as well as sociologists and research investigation teams have to be consulted in order to draft rules, tailored to the practical needs of consumers as weighted against the current economic climate in Europe.

Summary

In conclusion, co-operation on both central (European) and regional (national) level has to be encouraged in order to achieve a higher level of consumer protection and legal certainty. One should always take into consideration that the principles under the Smart Regulation, EU law and the legal traditions of member states are interdependent and interrelated; for this reason, there should be a smoother transition between them.

Annex I

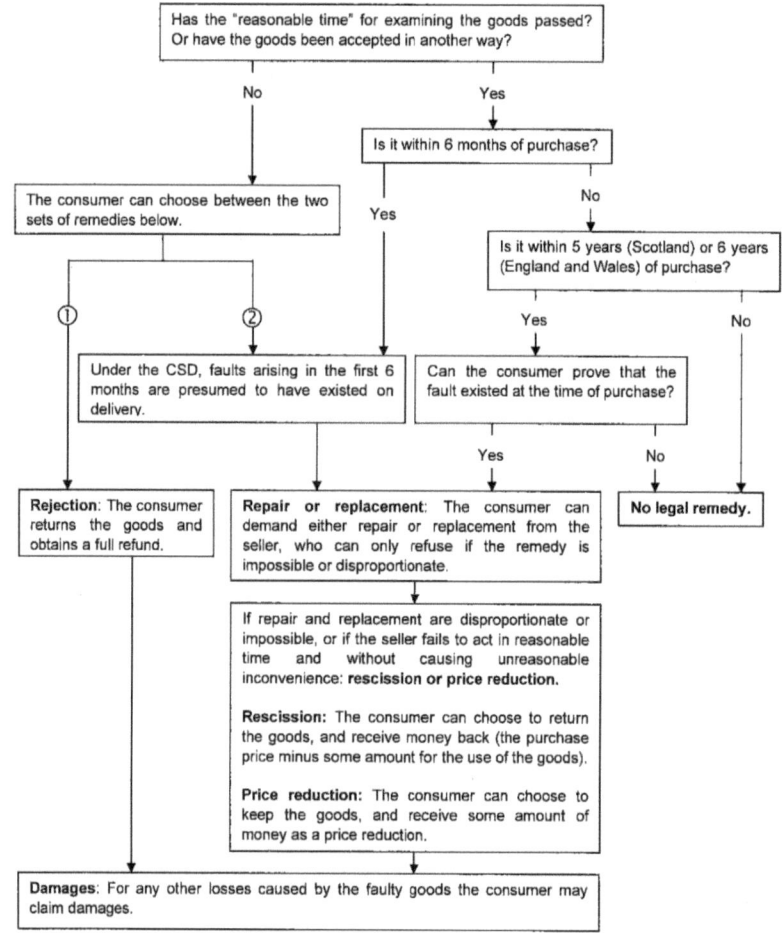

Source: Law Commission and Scottish Law Commission, *Consumer Remedies for Faulty Goods* (Law Com No 317, 2009), (SCOT Law Com No 216, 2009) 20.

Bibliography

Annex to Communication from the Commission to the European Parliament, the Council, the European Social and Economic Committee and the Committee of the Regions, 'Regulatory Fitness and Performance (REFIT): Results and Next Steps' COM (2013) 685 final <http://ec.europa.eu/smart-regulation/docs/20131002-refit-annex_en.pdf> (date accessed 12 March 2014).

Ardizzoni M., *German Tax and Business Law* (Sweet & Maxwell 2005).

Baskind E.et al, *Commercial Law* (Oxford University Press 2013).

Beckhaus G. K., *Die Rechtsnatur der Erfüllung: Eine Kritische Betrachtung der Erfüllungstheorien unter besonderer Berücksichtigung der Schuldrechtsmodernisierung* (Mohr Siebeck 2012).

Benöhr I., *EU Consumer Law and Human Rights* (Oxford University Press 2013).

Bernstein v Pamson Motors (Golders Green) Limited [1987] 2 All ER 220.

BGH Az. VIII ZR 226/11 (17.11.2012).

BGH VIII ZR 70/08 (21.12.2011).

Bradgate R. and White F., *Commercial Law 2012: LPC Guide* (Oxford University Press 2012).

Bürgerliches Geseztbuch 2002 [BGB].

Bussani M. and Werro F., *European private law* (Stämpfli Publishers 2001).

Campell D., *Remedies for International Sellers of Goods [2009] – II* (Yorkhill Law Publishing 2009).

Case C-404/06 *Quelle AG v Bundesverband der Verbraucherzentralen und Verbraucherverbände, European Court of Justice, Judgment* [2008] ECR I-2685.

Commission Staff Working Document on Monitoring and Consultation on Smart Regulation for SMEs, accompanying the document 'Smart Regulation - Responding to the needs of small and medium-sized enterprises' COM (2013) 122 final, <http://www.eumonitor.eu/9353000/1/j4nvgs5kjg27kof_j9vvik7m1c3gyxp/vj7s8q3qcfx0/f=/7268_13_add_1.pdf> (date accessed 12 March 2014).

Communication from the Commission to the European Parliament, the Council, the European Social and Economic Committee and the Committee of the Regions, EU Regulatory Fitnes, COM(2012) 746 final <http://ec.europa.eu/smart-regulation/better_regulation/documents/com_2013_en.pdf> (date accessed 12 March 2014).

Communication from the Commission to the European Parliament, the Council, the European Social and Economic Committee and the Committee of the Regions, 'Regulatory Fitness and Performance (REFIT): Results and Next Steps' COM (2013) 685 final <http://ec.europa.eu/smart-regulation/docs/20131002-refit_en.pdf> (date accessed 12 March 2014)

Consolidated Version of the Treaty on European Union (2008) OJ C 115/13.

Consumer Rights Bill HC Bill (2013-14) [161].

Cygan A., *Accountability, Parliamentarism and Transparency in the EU* (Edward Elgar Publishing 2013).

Deutscher Bundestag, 'Entwurf eines Gesetzes zur Umsetzung der Verbraucherrechterichtlinie und zur Änderung des Gesetzes zur Regelung der Wohnungsvermittlung' (2013) Drucksache 17/12637, 17. Wahlperiode.

--- 'Gesetzentwurf der Bundesregierung Entwurf eines Gesetzes zur Modernisierung des Schuldrechts' (2001) Drucksache 14-6857, 14. Wahlperiode.

--- 'Entwurf eines Gesetzes zur Modernisierung des Schuldrechts' (2001) Drucksache 14/6040, 14. Wahlperiode.

Directive 1999/44/EC of the European Parliament and of the Council of 25 May 1999 on certain aspects of the sale of consumer goods and associated guarantees OJ L 171 <http://eur-

lex.europa.eu/LexUriServ/LexUriServ.do?uri=CELEX:31999L0044:en:HTML> (date accessed 20 March 2014).

Directive 2000/31/EC of the European Parliament and of the Council of 8 June 2000 on certain legal aspects of information society services, in particular electronic commerce, in the internal market L 178 OJ <http://eur-lex.europa.eu/LexUriServ/LexUriServ.do?uri=CELEX:32000L0031:en:HTML> (date accessed 12 April 2014).

Directive 2000/35/EC of the European Parliament and the Council of 29 June 2000 on combating late payment in commercial transactions L 200/35 OJ < http://eur-lex.europa.eu/LexUriServ/LexUriServ.do?uri=OJ:L:2000:200:0035:0038:en:PDF> (date accessed 12 March 2014).

Directive 2005/29/EC of the European Parliament and of the Council of 11 May 2005 concerning unfair business-to-consumer commercial practices in the internal market and amending Council Directive 84/450/EEC, Directives 97/7/EC, 98/27/EC and 2002/65/EC of the European Parliament and of the Council and Regulation (EC) No 2006/2004 of the European Parliament and ofthe Council OJ L 290 <http://eur-lex.europa.eu/legal-content/en/ALL/?uri=CELEX:32005L0029> (date accessed 10 March 2014).

Directive 2011/83/EU of the European Parliament and of the Council of 25 October 2011 on consumer rights, amending Council Directive 93/13/EEC and Directive 1999/44/EC of the European Parliament and of the Council and repealing Council Directive 85/577/EEC and Directive 97/7/EC of the European Parliament and of the Council OJ L 304 <http://eur-lex.europa.eu/legal-content/EN/TXT/PDF/?uri=CELEX:32011L0083&rid=1> (date accessed 10 March 2014).

Emmerich V., *BGB-Schuldrecht Besonderer Teil* (C.F. Müller 2012).

European Commission, 'Report from the Commission on subsidiarity and proportionality' COM (2010) 547 final < http://eur-lex.europa.eu/LexUriServ/LexUriServ.do?uri=COM:2010:0547:FIN:EN:PDF> (accessed 12 March 2014).

--- 'Smart regulation: ensuring that European laws benefit people and businesses' (2010) IP/10/1296 < http://europa.eu/rapid/press-release_IP-10-1296_en.htm> (accessed 14 March 2014).

--- 'Better Regulation – simply explained' (2006) <http://ec.europa.eu/smart-regulation/better_regulation/documents/brochure/brochure_en.pdf> (date accessed 12 March 2014).

--- 'Green Paper on Guarantees for Consumer Goods and After-sales Services' COM (1993) 509 final.

Faust F.,'Das Kaufrecht im Vorschlag für ein Gemeinsames Europäisches Kaufrecht' in Schulte-Nölke H et al (ed), *Der Entwurf für ein optionales europäisches Kaufrecht* (Selier European law Publishers 2012).

Gillespie A., *The English Legal System* (Oxford University Press 2013).

Huber U. in BMJ (ed), *Gutachten und Vorschläge zur Überarbetung des Schulrechts* (Bundesanzeiger Verlag, 1981).

Huxley-Binns R., Martin J., *Unlocking the English Legal System* (Routledge 2014).

Jaeger A.-V. and Hök G.-S., *FIDIC - A Guide for Practitioners: A Guide for Practitioners* (Springer 2010).

Jaensch M., *Grundzüge des Bürgerlichen Rechts: mit 63 Fällen und Lösungen* (C.F. Müller 2012).

Jafarzadeh M., 'Buyer's Right to Specific Performance' in Maggi M. (ed), *Review of the Convention on Contracts for the International Sale of Goods (CISG) 2002-2003* (Kluwer Law International 2004).

Joined Cases C-6/90 and C-9/90 *Andrea Francovich v Italian Republic and Danila Bonifaci and Others and Italian Republic, Court of the European Union* [1991] ECR I-5375.

Joined Cases C-65/09 and C-97/09 *Gebr.Weber GmbH v Jürgen Wittmer, and Ingrid Putz v Medianess Electronics GmbH* [2011] ECR I-5257.

Jones L., *Introduction to Business Law* (Oxford University Press 2013).

Kaczorowska A., *European Union Law* (Routledge 2013).

Keenan D. J. and Smit K., *Smith & Keenan's Law for Business* (Longman 2006).

Kowalsky W. and Scherrer P. (ed), *Trade unions for a change of course in Europe* (ETUI 2011).

Lange M. et al, *Sachversicherungen für private und gewerbliche Kunden Fach- und Führungskompetenz für die Assekuranz* (Verlag Versicherungswirtschaft 2014).

Law Commission, *Limitation of Actions* (Law Com No 270, 2001).

--- Appendix D 'Comparative Consumer Law' <http://lawcommission.justice.gov.uk/docs/apd_website.pdf> (accessed 12 March 2014).

--- *Impact Assessment of Consumer Remedies for Faulty Goods* (2009) < http://lawcommission.justice.gov.uk/docs/lc317_impact.pdf> (accessed 12 March 2014).

Law Commission and Scottish Law Commission, *Consumer Remedies for Faulty Goods* (Law Com No 317, 2009), (SCOT Law Com No 216, 2009).

--- *Consumer Remedies For Faulty Goods: A Joint Consultation Paper* (Law Com CP No 188, 2009), (Scot Law Com DP No 139, 2009).

Le Goff P., *Die Vertragsstrafe in internationalen Verträgen zur Errichtung von Industrieanlagen* (Tanea 2005).

Limitation Act 1980.

Lisbon European Council, *Presidency Conclusions* (2000) < http://www.europarl.europa.eu/summits/lis1_en.htm> (accessed 12 March 2014).

Löwisch M., 'New Law of Obligations in Germany' 20 Ritsumeikan Law Review 141.

MacLeod J., *Consumer Sales Law* (Cavendish Publishing Limited 2002).

MacQueen H., 'Europeanization of Contract Law' in DiMatteo L. et al (ed), *Commercial Contract Law: Transatlantic Perspectives* (Cambridge University Press 2013).

MacQueen H. et al, 'Specific Performance and the Right to Cure' in Dannemann G. and Vogenauer S. (ed), *The Common European Sales Law in Context: Interactions with English and German law* (Oxford University Press 2013).

Magnus U., 'Consumer sales and associated guarantees' in Twigg-Flesner C. (ed), *The Cambridge Companion to European Union Private Law* (Cambridge University Press 2010).

Mandelkern Group on Better Regulation, Final Report (2001) < http://ec.europa.eu/smart-regulation/better_regulation/documents/mandelkern_report.pdf> (accessed 15 March 2014).

Meiers T., *Die Entwicklung und Reform der Sachmängelhaftung des Verkäufers beim Stückkauf* (Peter Lang GmbH 2010).

Micklitz H-W., 'Federal Order of Competence and Private Law' in Azoulai L.(ed), *The Question of Competence in the European Union* (Oxford University Press 2014).

Miller L., *The Emergence of EU Contract Law: Exploring Europeanization* (Oxford University Press 2011).

Moens G. and Trone J., *Commercial Law of the European Union* (Springer 2010).

Poole J., *Textbook on Contract Law* (Oxford University Press 2014).

Pott, P., 'Harmonising Different Rights of Withdrawal: Can German Law Serve as an Example for EC Consumer Law?' (2006) 7(12) German Law Journal 1109.

--- 'German Sales Law Two Years After the Implementation of Directive 1999/44/EC' (2004) 5 German Law Journal

237<http://www.germanlawjournal.com/pdf/Vol05No03/PDF_Vol_05_No_03_237-255_Private_Rott.pdf> (date accessed 14 March 2014).

--- 'Minimum Harmonisation for the Completion of the Internal Market? The Example of Consumer Sales Law' (2003) 40 CML Rev 1107.

Proposal for a directive on consumer rights, COM (2008) 614 final <http://ec.europa.eu/consumers/rights/cons_acquis_en.htm> (date accessed 14 March 2014).

Pott P. and Twigg-Flesner C., 'No Closer to Harmonisation? The Implementation of Directive 1999/44/EC into English and German Law Three Years On' in Howells G. et al, *The Yearbook of Consumer Law 2007* (Publisher 2007).

Prosser T., *The Regulatory Enterprise: Government, Regulation, and Legitimacy* (Oxford University Press 2010).

Ramjohn M., *Beginning Equity and Trusts* (Routledge 2013).

Reich N., 'Protection of Consumers' Economic Interests by EC Contract Law — Some Follow-up Remarks' (2006) 28 Sydney Law Review 37.

Rösler H., *Europäische Gerichtsbarkeit auf dem Gebiet des Zivilrechts* (Mohr Siebeck 2012).

Rott P., 'Technical Harmonization' versus Substantive Differences' in Somma A., *The Politics of the Draft Common Frame of Reference* (Kluwer Law International 2009).

Ryder N. et al, *Commercial Law: Principles and Policy* (Cambridge University Press 2012).

Sale of Goods Act 1979 [SoGA].

Scheck H. and Scheck B., *Wirtschaftliches Grundwissen: Für Naturwissenschaftler und Ingenieure* (JohnWiley & Sons 2012).

Schubert F., *Introduction to Law and the Legal System* (Cengage Learning 2014).

Shiomi Y., 'Modernization of German Civil Law' in Kitagawa Z. and Riesenhuber K. (ed), *The Identity of German and Japanese Civil Law in Comparative Perspectives/Die Identität des Deutschen und des Japanischen Zilivrechts in vergleichender Betrachtung* (De Gruyter Rechtswissenschaften Verlags – GmbH 2007).

The Draft 'Consumer Rights Bill' HC Bill (2013-2014) [697-I].

The Office of Fair Trading (OFT), 'Consumer Detriment: Assessing the frequency and impact of consumer problems with goods and services' (2008) OFT 992.

Treaty on European Union, as amended by the Maastricht Treaty (1992) OJ C 191.

Truk (UK) Limited v Tokmakidis GmbH [2000] 2 All ER (Comm) 594.

Twigg-Flesner C., *The Europeanisation of Contract Law: Current Controversies in Law* (Routledge 2013).

---   'Fit for purpose? The Proposals on Sales' in Howells G. and Schulze R. (ed), *Modernising and Harmonising Consumer Contract Law* (Selier Europeal Law Publishers 2009).

Weatherill S., *EU Consumer Law and Policy* (Eldar Publishing Limited 2013).

---   'Maximum versus Minimum Harmonization: Choosing between Unity and Diversity in the Search of the Soul of the Internal Market' in Shuibhne N. and Gormley L. (ed), *From Single Market to Economic Union: Essays in Memory of John A. Usher* (Oxford University Press 2012).

---   'Interpretation of the Directives: The Role of the Court' in Hartkamp A. et al (ed), *Towards a European Civil Code* (Kluwer Law International 2011).

---   'Consumer Policy' in Craig P.P. and De Búrca G. (ed), *The Evolution of EU Law* (Oxford University Press 2011).

---   *EU Consumer Law and Policy* (Elgar Publishing Limited 2005).

Wheeler J., *Essentials of the English Legal System* (Pearson Education Limited 2006).

Zimmermann R., 'Characteristic Aspects of German Legal Culture' in Reimann M. and Zekoll J., *Introduction to German law* (Kluwer Law International 2005).

--- *The Law of Obligations: Roman Foundation of the Civilian Tradition* (Clarendon Press 1996).

Zelst B. van, *The Politics of European Sales Law: A Legal-political Inquiry Into the the drafting of the Uniform Commercial Code, the Vienna Sales Convention, the Dutch Civil Code and the European Consumer Sales Directive in the context of the Europeanisation of contract law* (Kluwer Law International 2008).

Zumbansen P., 'The Law of Contracts' in Reimann M. and Zekoll J. (ed), *Introduction to German Law* (Kluwer Law International 2005).

Zwarg C., *Der Nacherfüllungsanspruch im BGB aus der Sicht eines verständigen Käufers* (Peter Lang GmbH 2010).

About the author

Zlatka Koleva is born in 1992 in Plovdiv, Bulgaria. After an excellent performance at Plovdiv English Language High School with majors in German, English, Bulgarian and Mathematics, she moved to Groningen, the Netherlands, to study a bachelor programme in International and European Law.

Throughout her studies she participated in the Erasmus Mundus programme and studied a semester at the University of Sheffield, UK, where Zlatka developed a passion for company and commercial law. This has inspired her to conduct a research in consumer law, which resulted in a comprehensive comparative study between the English legal system and the German law of obligations.

Currently, Zlatka is a Master student in Commercial law, specialization Commercial and Company law at Erasmus University Rotterdam.